BELAIR LESSON BANK

Forms of Poetry 1

Fred Sedgwick

Contents

Introduction	3
Humorous poetry	4
Poetry that plays with language	8
Riddles	12
Haiku	16
Cinquains	20
Couplets	24
List poems	28
Shape poems	32
Conversation poems	36
Epitaphs	40
Free verse	44
Glossary	48

Acknowledgements

Sunday morning in autumn

Autumn morning. Leaves
fall. Bells ring out endlessly.
Branches poke outwards.

Christopher, age 9

First published 2000 by Belair Publications.
United Kingdom: Belair Publications, Albert House, Apex Business Centre, Boscombe Road, Dunstable, LU5 4RL.

Belair allows photocopying of pages marked 'copiable page' for educational use, providing that this use is within the confines of the purchasing institution. Copiable pages should not be declared in any return in respect of any photocopying licence.

© 2000 Belair Publications, on behalf of the author.

Belair books are protected by international copyright laws. All rights are reserved. The copyright of all materials in this book, except where otherwise stated, remains the property of the publisher and author. No part of this publication may be reproduced, stored in a retrieval system, or transmitted, in any form or by any means, for whatever purpose, without the written permission of Belair Publications.

Editor: Terry Vittachi
Layout artist: Suzanne Ward
Cover design: Martin Cross
Illustrations: Lee Sullivan and Kirsty Wilson

Every effort has been made to contact copyright holders of material used in this book. If any have been overlooked, we will be pleased to make any necessary arrangements.

British Library Cataloguing in Publication Data. A catalogue record for this book is available from the British Library.

Fred Sedgwick hereby asserts his moral right to be identified as the author of this work in accordance with the Copyright, Designs and Patents Act 1988.

ISBN 1 84191 047-3

Introduction

Forms of Poetry 1 is one of a series of books designed to help children enjoy poetry while they learn about its many forms. Poetry is arguably unique in its ability to stretch and challenge children because, by its very nature, it differs from the prose fiction and non-fiction which forms the bulk of their reading; it introduces children to new, exciting, dynamic forms of creativity and self-expression, using a wide variety of poetic devices from traditional rhyme to free verse. The series aims to stimulate a lifelong interest in and appreciation of poetry, encourage children to compose their own poems, and motivate them to seek out new favourite writers of their own, extending their reading and developing a new perspective on their relationship with language. Many of the poems featured in the books are written by children, letting your class see what children are capable of and inspiring them to similar heights.

The structure of the book

Forms of Poetry 1 explores a variety of poem formats to help children learn to appreciate poetry and stimulate them to write poems of their own.

Each chapter is designed to give ideas for class, group and individual work, following a similar pattern. The poetry sheet features one or more poems, which can be photocopied. Ideally you will introduce the poem, and either you or one or more of the children will read it aloud. This could be followed by some initial discussion exploring how each poem achieves its effect, and encouraging the children to develop their own thoughts for the theme.

The children can then move on to the activity sheets, either in groups or individually. The activities allow the children to think about the poem, experiment and play with words, and brainstorm their ideas. Sometimes the children are asked to write their own poems; further suggestions for written work are also given. Some of the chapters include suggestions for performing the poems.

General principles

- Offer your own ideas, but make sure you lay claim to them. Say something like 'You can't use that, because I thought of it, but I'm sure you can think of something even better.'

- Handwriting, spelling and grammar are not vital at the stage when the children are making their notes. This is the 'first draft' stage, where the main objective is for the children to get their ideas down into note form which they can read. They will be buzzing with ideas, and you do not want to impede their creativity. When the final version is made, you can attend to the technical aspects.

- The five senses are vital to vivid poetry. 'What can you hear/smell/see/touch/taste?' are always useful questions.

- You and the children should play with the poems: recite them in different ways, and have fun with them.

Glossary

There is a short glossary of useful terms at the end of the book.

Belair Lesson Banks on CD

All Belair *Lesson Banks* come in a CD format as well as book format. The CDs offer the children the opportunity to work on a computer, a learning tool they often find stimulating, while working through the same high quality activities found in the book.

Key features
- The discs have many activities on them including responding to pictures, writing frames, working in tables, sorting and matching activities, and scored 'multi-choice' questions.

- Many of the activities can be altered. If you, as the teacher, want to modify the language or change a question, you can do so easily. You can make changes such as:
  - simplify the text
  - add complexity to the language and structure
  - provide model answers or examples.
- Many screens have a linked screen which gives the children an opportunity to write an extended piece in response to a question. The linked screen will automatically print out with the original screen.
- Finally, you can of course modify the activities on screen and print them out for the children to use as paper activities.

ideas page

Humorous poetry

Introduction

Humour depends on individual perceptions, but some elements of comedy are clearly identifiable. One such element is the surprise ending, and this features in *Not a word*, where the meek heroine turns out to be bovine in every sense of the word. Again, slapstick is a recognised comic element, and this is demonstrated in *Deborah Delora*. The humour from the final poem comes from the reversal of the expected situation, where the title is lengthy and the poem breathtakingly brief. At least one of these poems should appeal to you and your class!

Learning Objectives

- To appreciate humour in poetry, especially the critical element of surprise.
- To write a funny prose anecdote that could be made into a poem.
- To understand that the first draft of a poem can begin as prose.

Discussion

- Talk with the children about what makes them laugh. They may mention incidents at home, or they may talk about a television programme; try to help them identify exactly what they find funny, mentioning elements of comedy such as surprise, slapstick and so on.
- Discuss jokes and the nature of the punchline, which hinges on the element of surprise. Try telling them this one, or something similar, as a lead-in:
  Bill: *I've got a new pet.*
  Jill: *Where are you going to keep it?*
  Bill: *In my bedroom.*
  Jill: *What about the smell?*
  Bill: *Oh, it'll soon get used to that.*
- Extend the discussion to what surprises the children and ask them to give some examples; mention other examples of humour with a surprise ending, or where they can foresee a surprise ending when the subject of the tale cannot: can they sympathise with a turkey who is invited for Christmas dinner?

Activity Pages

A twist in the tale ...
Encourage the children to write as much detail as possible. They can write either a story or a poem, but the poems need not rhyme.

Unexpected endings
Make sure the children understand that what is funny in a joke or story may not be amusing in real life; slipping on a banana skin, for example, can be painful. Discuss why the naughtiness of the children in the exercise is humorous, and ask them for ideas about what they think constitutes 'naughty' behaviour. Did they do anything as small children that they would recognise as naughty now? Do they do anything now that they know is naughty?

Written Work

- Ask the children to write a poem that has a very long title, but a very short text.
- Ask the children to make a note of something very naughty that they remember doing, or that they remember their brothers or sisters doing. Ask them to write the story down, making sure that they keep a surprise for the end. Ask them to arrange the story in free verse (see page 44 for more details on free verse).
- Ask the children to write a free verse poem about a naughty animal: for example, a monkey throwing something nasty in a zoo, a mischievous puppy, a new kitten and so on.

Performance Ideas

Not a word lends itself well to reading aloud, and the children could experiment with different voices. A romantic tone could be used for the beginning, followed by a pause before the final dénouement. Challenge the children to read *Deborah Delora* aloud in a variety of ways to bring out the humour; they could use the voice of a disapproving adult, an admiring child and so on. The third poem could be performed at an assembly, with one person reading out the title, and the rest of the class shouting out the one-word punchline 'poem'.

Humorous poetry

Poetry page

Not a word

They walked the lane together.
The sky was dotted with stars.
They reached the rails together.
He lifted up the bars.
She neither smiled nor thanked him,
Because she knew not how –
For he was the farmer's boy
And she was a Jersey cow.

Anon

Deborah Delora

Deborah Delora, she liked a bit of fun.
She went to the baker's and she bought a penny bun,
Dipped the bun in treacle and threw it at the teacher –
Deborah Delora! What a wicked creature!

Anon

What the Headteacher said when he saw me running out of school on June 21 last year to buy an ice cream from Pelozzi's van

Hey!*

Fred Sedgwick

*This poem has been lodged with the **Guinness Book of Records** as the shortest poem in the world.

A twist in the tail ...

Read *Not a word* on the poetry page. The ending is a surprise, and that's what makes it funny. Look at the pictures here. They tell stories with unexpected endings, too. Tell the stories in your own words, writing about everything that happens in each picture.

 Write a story or a poem of your own with a twist in the tale – an unexpected ending! If you can't think of anything, try one of these ideas: a ghost who is afraid of the dark; a dragon who wants to be a fire-fighter; a vegetarian vulture.

Unexpected endings

Read *Deborah Delora* on the poetry page. Then look at these pictures of children doing things they shouldn't ...

Little Susie Spooner liked to stir things up.

Naughty Norman Nailer liked to make a noise.

Teeny tiny animals were Tina Tindall's love.

Finicky Freddie Fedora loved to make a fuss.

Choose one picture and write a story about it. The first line is done for you. Try to think of an unexpected ending!

Think of the naughtiest thing you can imagine, and write a story or a poem about it. Draw a picture to illustrate your work.

© Belair (copiable page)   BELAIR LESSON BANK – Forms of Poetry 1

ideas page — Poetry that plays with language

Introduction

This chapter deals with alliteration and puns. Most children will quickly grasp the concept of alliteration and have fun with it. Puns, however, are not so easy! The **Folens Dictionary and Thesaurus** defines a pun as 'a kind of joke that uses two words that sound the same but have different meanings.' Perhaps the best way to help the children to understand the concept is to make some puns yourself. You may want to arm yourself with a supply from a joke book beforehand.

Learning Objectives

- To introduce the idea of playing with language.
- To focus specifically on alliteration, puns and onomatopoeia.

Discussion

- Alliteration is a relatively simple concept, and the children can have fun making up their own alliterative sentences. Start them off with some examples, such as *Down in the dungeon demons dreamt of danger*.
- Ask the children to think of some heavily alliterative sentences and write them down.
- Alliteration is not an intrinsically comic device, but most puns are meant to be funny and are therefore more challenging to devise. Give the children an example:
  Why did the coal scuttle?
  Because it saw the kitchen sink.
  Explain to the children that this joke contains two puns; one is the two meanings for scuttle, namely the noun meaning a coal container and the verb meaning to sink a ship; the second is the two meanings of 'sink', meaning a kitchen sink, and the verb meaning to go below the water. Use another pun to illustrate the use of words with similar sounds; this one depends on the similar sounds of 'mushroom' and 'much room':
  I've got some toadstools in my desk.
  How do you know they're toadstools?
  Because there's not mushroom inside.

Activity Pages

Rakesh ran like a rocket
Begin the activity by asking the children to make a list of nouns beginning with the same letter. Once they get started, they should realise that this is a simple matter. They could then write a list of verbs beginning with the same letter before progressing to writing alliterative sentences. Invite some of them to read their sentences out loud. Then begin the activity.

Playing with puns
Reiterate the main points from the class discussion on puns. While the children are completing the activity sheet, you may want to help some of them find these ones in the poem: 'tap', 'toe the line' and 'egg'.

Written Work

- Ask the children to write a non-rhyming alliterative poem; start them off with the following:
  A is an antelope that aims at Amy.
  B is a buzzard that builds with bricks.
  C is a cow that calls at cats.
  D is a dog that dribbles over daisies.
- Divide the class into groups and allocate them each a section of the alphabet, perhaps five or six letters. When they have finished, put all the sentences together and have the class perform it in an assembly.
- Ask the children to write another line for each stanza of the poem, like this:
      I used to go ballooning over Portugal
      but
      then I heard a POP!
      and
      I sank to the sand in Spain.
  Each ending should either be alliterative, or have a pun in it.
- Ask the children to write onomatopoeic sentences, with each line containing a word which sounds like its meaning, such as:
  – Bees buzzed around our picnic.
  – Gulls squawked overhead.

Poems that play with language

Poetry page

I used to go tap-dancing

I used to go tap-dancing
but
I tripped into the sink.

Once I was a star
but –
how sad! – I lost my sparkle.

I used to have a magical memory
but
now I …

Once I had perfect eyesight
but –
please, Peter, where are you?

I used to go ballooning over Portugal
but
then I heard a powerful POP.

Once my feet tripped into trouble every Tuesday
but
now I toe the line.

I used to make butterflies on Mars
but
now I make do with moths on Mercury.

I used to be a good boy
but
Humpty Dumpty egged me on.

Rakesh ran like a rocket

Read *I used to go tap-dancing* on the poetry page. Notice how each stanza, or verse, repeats one letter. This is called **alliteration**.

1. Find the repeated, or alliterative, letter in each stanza. Copy out three stanzas, with the repeated letter in a different colour.

2. Pick one of the repeated letters and write down 16 nouns beginning with that letter.

3. Write a sentence with one letter repeated at least three times. Try to use some of the words you wrote in the boxes.

_____

_____

4. Complete these sentences, repeating the first letter at least three times. Use a dictionary if you like.

| Rakesh ran like a rocket _____ |
| Tiny Timothy tipped _____ |
| Mary moodily muttered _____ |
| Snooty Sarah said _____ |

Write three more sentences, each repeating any letter that you choose.

Playing with puns

I used to go tap-dancing plays with the fact that a word can have two meanings. This kind of word-play is called a **pun**. Some jokes play with the way words sound. Knock-knock jokes use puns with words of similar sounds, like this one:

1. Read *I used to go tap-dancing* again. Can you find any puns in the poem? Use the pictures to help you, and make a note of them on a separate sheet.

2. Complete these captions using puns.

"Phew! I've laid seven eggs today!"
"You must be
Y ☐ ☐ K ☐ ☐ G!"

"I hope you aren't wearing your mummy out."
"Don't be silly. I'm
☐ ☐ ☐ R ☐ ☐ G
my new dress!"

"Why do you like bananas so much?"
"I don't know, they just
☐ P ☐ ☐ A ☐
to me."

 See if you can think of a pun of your own. Draw a cartoon to go with it.

Riddles

ideas page

Introduction

An expert on riddles, Kevin Crossley-Holland, writes that the misleading descriptions and mind-bending word-play of riddles are powerful because they contain secrets. The word 'secret' is important here, because children enjoy sharing and guessing secrets. The word 'riddle' comes from the Anglo-Saxon 'raedan', meaning to teach or instruct, and by means of jokes, puns and catch questions, a riddle teaches us about the subject of the riddle and the language in which the riddle is framed. There is playfulness in riddles too, which appeals to children.

Learning Objectives

- To use extended metaphors.
- To write riddles.

Discussion

What am I? and What are we?
Ask the children to look at the riddles in groups, with three of them taking turns to read them aloud. Then ask everybody, in secret, to write down what they think the answer is. Read each riddle to the class again yourself, and ask them to write down another possible answer. Then go over the riddles with the whole class, helping those who have not yet arrived at the answers. Finally, tell them the answers, which are a ladder and the vowels respectively.

A very large riddle
The answer to this is 'God'. Read the riddle to the class. 'Pews' are church benches, and 'study my worth' is a literal translation of the old word 'worship', literally 'worthship'. Others are worshipping their cars by washing them. Ask the children for different names of God such as Allah, Jehovah and Yahweh. The quarrels are religious conflicts, and 'cross' is a pun. The small black books are hymn books.

Who am I?
The answer to this is 'nothing'. Read the riddle to the class. It is a trick question which, once answered, explains itself. Point out to the children how the clue might have helped them.

Activity Pages

Writing a riddle
Take the children through the different ways of looking at a candle, then repeat the exercise with the pictures of the moon, asking the children to suggest what it looks like in the various stages. The illustrations suggest a man's face, the moon as a spinning satellite of the earth and the moon pulling on the sea to cause tides. Ask them for any other ideas they have about the moon, then ask them to write their moon riddle. When they compose their own riddle, have some subjects ready to suggest to anyone who cannot think of anything, such as a light bulb, a window, a chrysalis or a plant seed.

School riddles
Help the children to see the fun in riddles; emphasise their secret nature, and point out how they often feature in fantasy stories: if the hero or heroine can solve a riddle, they gain power in the story. Then take them through the activity page. **Answers:** globe, whistle, ceiling.

Written Work

Writing ideas
Help the children to use their ideas to complete their own riddles. The riddle should begin with either the word 'I' or the word 'My', or contain one of these words early on. Tell them that they are trying to play tricks on the reader, so the riddle should be quite difficult; anything which makes immediate sense is too easy! Mention puns, pointing out the pun on 'cross' in *A very large riddle*. You could suggest the children write riddles on aspects of their current topics in history or science. For example, a cloud: 'I weep on your land ...'

Performance Ideas

Ask the children to find some more riddles from teachers, family, books and friends in the playground. Make a class riddle collection and have the children read them aloud during an assembly. The riddles can be written up and displayed, with the answers on separate sheets on another wall; children can match the clues to the answers.

Riddles

Poetry page

Look at these riddles. Can you work them out? Use the clues!

What am I?

Up I step, and down,
making the longest side
of a right-angled
and unlucky triangle.
Without me
you would never hold
such a high view of the world.
I have rungs you cannot ring,
but am nothing like a bell.

Fred Sedgwick

Clues:
Rungs, but not a bell;
unlucky.

A very large riddle

You take a pew
to study my worth
while others adore
their cars in the Sabbath sun.

I have so many names,
so many natures,
and, quarrelling about them,
you cross me time and time again.

I am not small black books in a row.
I am the silent word
walking in the garden
in the cool of the day.

Fred Sedgwick

Clues:
Pew; Sabbath; cross.

What are we?

We are five little airy creatures,
All of different voice and features.
One of us in g**l**ass is set;
One of us you'll find in j**e**t;
T'other you may see in t**i**n;
And the fourth a b**o**x within;
If the fifth you should p**u**rsue,
It can never fly from you.

Jonathan Swift, 1667–1745

Clue:
Look at the letters in **bold**!

Who am I?

Rich men have none of me,
poor men have all of me.
I am greater than God
and more wicked than the devil.
I promise you this:
eat me, and you die.

Anon

Clue:
This is a trick question, really.
Nothing should make you cross when
your teacher tells you the answer!
Absolutely nothing!

Writing a riddle

Writing a riddle is easier than you think! Start by choosing a subject. Then look at it in a different way. Here is an example.

What is it?	What does it look like?	What does it do?	Anything else?

a candle is ...	a column ...	weeping waxen tears ...	while it slowly shrinks.

Now you have your riddle: I am a column. I slowly shrink as I weep my waxen tears. What am I?

Try writing your own riddle, using the pictures below.

What is it?	What does it look like?	What does it do?	Anything else?
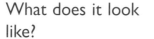			
the moon is ...			

 Write a riddle of your own. Pick one subject and look at it in different ways; then write about it. Draw a picture to go with it. (If you can't think of anything, here are some suggestions: the wind; a light bulb; a window.)

School riddles

1. Read these riddles and see if you can solve them.

Though I never speak,
I tell you roundly
about the third planet.

A cheap necklace,
I bring the playground to
　sudden order –
STAND STILL!!! –
with one blast.

From me hangs light.
Go any higher than me
and you're free in the clear
　air,
like a bird, or a plane, or,
　better still,
a new idea.

answer _____ answer _____ answer _____

2. Think hard about all the things in your school. You could write a riddle about almost any of them. Make a list of them in the table below. Two examples are given for you.

desk			
playground			

 Make up your own school riddle. It can be about anything to do with school. What about the school bell, or the teacher's register, or a pair of sweaty gym-shoes?

ideas page

Haiku

Introduction

Haiku are a traditional Japanese form of poetry. A haiku has 17 syllables, usually (but not always) with five in the first line, seven in the second and five in the third. Matsuo Basho (1644–1694) is one of the most famous poets who helped to develop the form. A traditional haiku captures a single impression of a natural object or scene and links it to the natural world. A contemporary haiku is often less philosophical and sometimes humorous.

Learning Objectives

- To count syllables.
- To write accurate haiku.

Discussion

- Haiku should contain two vivid images, and the seasons are especially suitable subjects for them. Go through the autumn haiku, pointing out that there does not need to be punctuation at the end of a line. Also point out that haiku have more than one image: leaves, bells and branches in the first; sun, fog, frost and bare trees in the last one. Then go through some place names with the children, counting syllables, and play syllable games with the children's names.
- You do not need to consider metre or rhyme with haiku. All that matters is the building up of the correct number of syllables. As you become more familiar with the format, you and the children will be able to predict the timing of the poems and to appreciate their inevitability.
- Point out that a haiku should contain an image that implies more than it says; for example, this hints at death:

    When the evening sun
    drops behind the busy street
    I think of endings.

  Other suitable subjects for haiku are weather, animals and flowers.

Activity Pages

Syllable sounds
This activity will help children explore syllables and focus on the syllable count of a haiku. Have some atlases and maps to hand. Go round the room as the children work, perhaps in pairs or groups, and help them to build their lists.

Place haiku
This activity will further assist the children in examining the structure of a haiku. Help the children arrange the names into place haiku. These haiku will clearly not have the two images characteristic of the format, and may be lacking in subtlety, but will help the children focus on how haiku are composed.

Written Work

- Ask the children to write a haiku about a season. You might collect words and images for your season on the blackboard first. For example, for spring you could have blossom, pink, green, bright, cuckoo or nests. Ask the children to read the haiku on the poetry page in groups to each other, checking the number of syllables in each one. Then ask them to write their own seasonal haiku. At the end of this, they will have written a haiku calendar which can be displayed.
- Oscar Wilde said: "I don't quote accurately. Anyone can quote accurately. I quote with great feeling." This can usefully be applied to haiku; a good haiku might have anything between ten and twenty syllables, but it will be interesting, so don't be too dogmatic about the syllable count.
  Do try to steer the children away from clichés. It is worth discussing clichés with children, because if they can eliminate them from their writing, they will make enormous strides forward. Give them some examples of what to avoid: birds 'tweeting' or blossoms 'smelling like perfume' or the use of 'nice' when something more vivid would convey a better description. Ask them 'What could you write instead that tells us more about your subject?'
- Ask the children to write a haiku about some of the subjects they looked at in the section on riddles, such as a candle, the moon or a ladder.

Haiku

Poetry page

Sunday morning in autumn

Autumn morning. Leaves
fall. Bells ring out endlessly.
Branches poke outwards.

Christopher, age 9

Autumn: a double haiku

Shafts of sunlight slip
through red, orange leaves dancing
to the sound of bells.

Leaves flutter to the
ground, like coloured snowflakes, and
crunch under your feet.

Shixin, age 10

Autumn haiku

Dim sun shines through fog.
Frost. Trees bare with red, orange,
Brown, yellow, scattered.

Thomas, age 10

© Belair (copiable page)   BELAIR LESSON BANK – Forms of Poetry 1   17

Syllable sounds

Syllables are the number of sounds a word makes. The place name Dublin has two syllables: Dub-lin.

1. Look at the place names below. Work out how many syllables are in each place name. Complete the table. An example has been done for you. Watch out for Edinburgh!

Windermere

Bath

Edinburgh

Newcastle upon Tyne

Name	Syllables	Sounds
Cardiff	two	Car-diff

 Look up 20 place names in an atlas. Then make a list of them. Divide the list into places with one syllable, places with two to four syllables, and places with five or more.

Place haiku

A haiku is a poem that has 17 syllables, arranged like this:

      5 in the first line   7 in the second   5 in the third.

You can use place names to make a haiku. Here are some examples.

Haiku of the Hebrides

Isle of Skye. Cross the
Little Minch. Uist and Lewis.
Distant St Kilda.

South London Haiku

Streatham Hill and Brix-
ton, Croydon, Norbury, Thorn-
ton Heath and Norwood.

Use some of the place names you have collected from an atlas. Write your own place haiku.

 Use the atlas to look up some place names in a country you have never been to, but would like to visit. Write your own haiku of places you would like to see one day. What about Disneyland? Or the North Pole?

ideas page

Cinquains

Introduction

The cinquain format was invented by the American poet, Adelaide Crapsey. Syllable counting has been covered in the chapter on haiku, but can be revised here if necessary. Cinquains are arranged in five lines with a syllabic structure of: 2,4,6,8,2. Usually a cinquain does not rhyme.

Learning Objectives

- To introduce the children to cinquains.
- To understand the impact and uses of short and long lines.
- To write cinquains.

Discussion

- Select and describe a number of objects in the room using a pattern similar to the description of the clock on the activity page. Ask the children to contribute to the description. Write one of the descriptions on the board, checking first that it is long enough to be divided up into a short line (under three syllables), a longer one (less than six syllables), a longer one still (six or more syllables), an even longer one (eight plus), and a very short one (less than three). Ask a child to do the same. Give them this example:

  Leeds. Hull.
  Arsenal and
  Rangers. Swansea City.
  Manchester United. Aston
  Villa.

- Read the four cinquain poems aloud, asking the children to count the syllables. Then work with the children to see if the description you have written on the board can be turned into a cinquain, removing and adding words as necessary.
- Ask the class whether they think cinquains lend themselves best to serious subjects, or whether they can think of a subject for a humorous cinquain. Can they see any advantages to writing a poem with a specific number of lines and syllables?

Activity Pages

Classroom cinquain
Reinforce the cinquain structure of line length and syllable count as you go through the example about the clock. Have some suggestions of possible topics ready for any children who require them.

Kale and cabbage cinquains
The work the children have done so far has focused on the shape and structure of the cinquain. This sheet asks them to write cinquains with the correct syllabic count, using lists of items of food. Before the children begin, ask them to read the poems on the poetry page to themselves again and count the number of syllables. Remind them of the work they have already done on syllables if necessary. The correct order of the two cinquains is:

Apple	2
Carrots and peas	4
Cauliflower, lettuce	6
Tomatoes bright red, all from my	8
Garden!	2
Ice cream	2
Chocolate sauce	4
Cream, nuts and fudge pieces	6
Tall glass, big spoon, wide smile, as I	8
Eat all!	2

Written Work

- Other suggestions for cinquain subjects are:
  The weather today   My cat
  The blackbird on the wall The quiet playground
  Sweets   Sports teams
  Historical names (perhaps Pop groups
  related to a current history topic)
- Add a new dimension to the lesson by showing the children this way of arranging cinquains; it will help them visualise how the line lengths work.

December cinquain
Rainbow
against lead in
the winter sky: a gull
floats on the wind. Starlings rest on
chimneys.

Sad family cinquain
My best friends: Mum, Dad. So
why oh why can't they be
friends with each other as they are
with me?

Cinquains

Poetry page

December cinquain

Rainbow
against lead in
the winter sky: a gull
floats on the wind. Starlings rest on
chimneys.

Fred Sedgwick

Love cinquain

I love
Gertie Jones' grin:
her eyes, laughter-bright; how
she smiles. The way she laughs; giggles ...
Loves me!

Fred Sedgwick

Sad family cinquain

My best
friends: Mum, Dad. So
why oh why can't they be
friends with each other as they are
with me?

Fred Sedgwick

Christmas cinquain

Christmas
comes again with
meaning behind wine and
glittering tinsel sparkling: that
Baby.

Fred Sedgwick

Classroom cinquain

Look at this sentence:

> The red clock's hands, except one, invisibly move and the day goes by: morning, mid-day, afternoon. And soon I will go home.

This sentence can be divided into lines of different lengths:

> The red
> clock's hands, except one,
> invisibly move and the day goes by:
> morning, mid-day, afternoon. And soon I will
> go home.

Look around the room and pick any object you like. Now write a sentence about it. Split it up into lines of different lengths, like the example above.

 Find something else in the room to write about. On a separate sheet, write a poem about it with five lines of different length. Decorate your page with drawings to go with your poem.

Kale and cabbage cinquains

A cinquain is a poem with five lines. Each line has a set number of syllables, arranged like this:

2 in the first line **4** in the second **6** in the third **8** in the fourth **2** in the fifth.

Here is an example. Do you like these foods? They're very good for you!

Brussels	2
sprouts. Parsnips. Greens,	4
spinach, cabbage, kale and	6
broccoli, hardly cooked; and, wow!	8
green beans!	2

Here are two cinquains about different kinds of foods. The lines have been jumbled up. Work out how many syllables there are in each line. Then cut out the lines and rearrange them into the right order to make two cinquains. Write the cinquains out on a separate sheet of paper and draw a picture to go with each one.

Cinquain line	No. of syllables
Tall glass, big spoon, wide smile, as I	
Carrots and peas	
Cream, nuts and fudge pieces	
Ice cream	
Tomatoes bright red, all from my	
Garden!	
Chocolate sauce	
Apple	
Eat all!	
Cauliflower, lettuce	

 Write down a list of your favourite foods and make it into a cinquain. If you have lots of favourites, write two cinquains!

ideas page

Couplets

Introduction

This exercise introduces children to writing couplets and specifically to writing rhyming poetry. Although most children can readily understand the concept of rhymes, they may find them difficult to write. Here they will learn the importance of metre in rhyme, and also the importance of meaning; in other words, the words put in to make the rhyme must also have relevance to the content, and not just be included for the sake of their sound.

Learning Objectives

- To understand and write couplets.
- To consider the function of rhyme.

Discussion

- Read *Mr Khan's shop* aloud, emphasising the internal rhymes based on 'ah'. They are: dark, parathas, masala, naan, bhajis, dal, garlic, darkens, Khan. Point out that the poem is like a list. (List poems will be studied in detail in the next chapter.)
- Discuss the term 'stanza', explaining that a stanza is to a poem as a verse is to a song. Find another poem in rhyming couplets, and talk about the way each couplet forms a stanza. Alternatively, use this example:

  Sarah, Sharif, Jerlisa and Jo
  play near the path where the roses grow.

  Hannah, Hussain and Humphrey hold hands.
  Sipping her coffee, Miss Southern stands.

  (From *Friends at playtime*, Fred Sedgwick)

- Read *Unicorns* aloud, this time emphasising the rhyming words at the end of the lines. You may want to read out some other examples of couplets.

Activity Pages

Food couplets
Before they begin, divide the children into groups and ask them to make lists of different foods. Then ask them to write brief descriptions of those foods.

Rhyming couplets
Discuss words that do not rhyme, ensuring the children appreciate the difference. The children should understand that rhyming words in poems must contribute to the meaning, and fit in with the metre. The children should have fun thinking of rhyming words. If they need extra encouragement, here are some suggestions to start them off:

too: blue, screw, pew, mew, through

crow: blow, flow, grow, go, no (and know), so, sew, mow

flea: plea, tea (and tee), Brie, tree, she, me, bee, fee

bright: night, plight, fight, bite, might, kite, light, height

school: fool, tool, mule, cool, drool

Help them build up lists of rhyming words, and help them find rhymes for their first names as required.

Written Work

- Ask the children to write a rhyming couplet (using their lists from the sheet 'Rhyming couplets'), with the added challenge of observing the following conditions:
  - the rhyme must follow a metre;
  - the lines must be the same length;
  - the rhyme must have genuine meaning.
- Ask the children to write a poem about their favourite foods in a poem of couplets without traditional rhymes, as in *Mr Khan's shop*. Suggest that they include a personality in the poem, like Mr Khan. Some cookery books may be helpful here, or an in-depth knowledge of supermarket shelves and brands of, for example, biscuits or crisps.

Couplets

Poetry page

Mr Khan's shop

is dark and beautiful.
There are parathas,

garam masala,
naan breads full of fruit.

There are bhajis, samosas,
dhal, garlic, ground cumin seeds.

Shiny emerald chillies
lie like incendiary bombs.

There are bhindi in sacks,
aloo to eat with hot puris

and mango pickle. There's
rice, yogurt,

cucumber and mint –
raita to cool the tongue.

Sometimes you see,
where the shop darkens,

Mr Khan, his wife
and their children

round the table.
The smells have come alive.

He serves me
poppadoms, smiles,

re-enters the dark.
Perhaps one day

he'll ask me to dine with
them: bhajis, samosas, pakoras,

coriander, dhal.
I'll give him this poem: "Sit down,

young man", he'll say
"and eat your words."

Fred Sedgwick

Unicorns

My mate, Mickey McNay,
Made friends with a unicorn today.

Leela and Tara, the twins,
Are angels pirouetting on pins.

Maria Memento, because of a smell,
Is a memory deep in an African well.

But the magic you and I make
We build in dreams, asleep, awake ...

and the dream may be poem or prayer.
Just listen. It will be there.

Fred Sedgwick

Food couplets

Look at the poems on the poetry page. One rhymes and one does not, but both are written in couplets. A couplet is a verse of two lines.

Read *Mr Khan's shop*. Choose three foods from the poem, and write a couplet of your own about each of them.

My food:_____

_____

_____

My food:_____

_____

_____

My food:_____

_____

_____

Although *Mr Khan's shop* doesn't rhyme, it has lots of 'ah' sounds in it, like the 'ah' sounds in dark and masala. Find other long 'ah' sounds in this poem and write them down.

Rhyming couplets

1. Read *Unicorns* on the poetry page. Then look at the list below. Find a word in the poem to rhyme with each word in the list. Then think of another rhyming word of your own. The first one is done for you.

Word in poem	Rhyming word in poem	My rhyming word
McNay	today	play
twins		
smell		
make		
prayer		

2. Find two rhymes for each of the words below. The first one is done for you.

too	blue	you
crow		
flea		
bright		
school		

3. Add two more words of your own and find rhymes for them.

Write down your first name. Then write down as many rhymes for it as you can think of. If you can't think of any, ask a friend or your teacher! Then write a rhyming couplet using your name.

ideas page

List poems

Introduction

Most children will find list poems fun and relatively easy to write, once they are under way. Have a brainstorming session, where the children can suggest and list anything that comes to mind. Reluctant writers can be encouraged to think of ten cars, or twelve football teams, or fifteen names of pop singers. The children should be encouraged to write their ideas quickly, in any order, then select the best items on their list, and finally order the items into a list poem.

Learning Objectives

- To introduce the concept of list poems.
- To write a list poem.

Discussion

- A good way to start discussing list poems is to begin with a list the children are familiar with: a shopping list. Write one on the board with the children's help, leaving gaps between each item. Then go back over the list, filling in the gaps with more details, inviting suggestions from the class. For example, if orange squash features on the list, encourage supplementary lines from the children such as 'for me and my brother at dinnertime'. You could extend this to shopping lists that a cat might make, or a dragon, or a wizard, or someone from your current historical topic such as a Viking or a Roman. This is a good opportunity to emphasise the fun in poetry. Ask the children to imagine a Viking supermarket, for example.
- Another useful 'listing' exercise is to discuss lists of different items within groups, particularly natural objects, such as a list of trees, dinosaurs, mammals and so on.
- Discuss repetition, referring to *There is in me*, and the subtle way rhymes appear in *The children that I know*. Ask them to listen out for and point out the rhymes which they may not take in on first hearing.

Activity Pages

Writing lists
This activity encourages the children to write lists of their own, and add more, as they have begun to do as a class. It also encourages the children to consider their own likes and dislikes. The children could work in groups for this activity, perhaps swapping lists to add more lines.

There is in me
This activity encourages a creative flow of lists by focusing on the roles children play inside their heads and the different moods they have. Read them this further example of a mood poem:

> There is in me
> The cheer of Louis' jazz
> in New Orleans.
> There is in me
> the shout of the home crowd
> when we score.
> There is also in me,
> though,
> a black cloud, sometimes
> pouring rain on people…

Written Work

- Ask the children to choose one of their 'brainstorming' lists and make it into a list poem, encouraging them to select and edit so that they are aware of the different stages involved in the evolution of a poem.
- Ask the children to write another list poem connected to their current science or history topic, such as electricity, the Tudors, dinosaurs or the Second World War, as appropriate.
- As a follow-up to *There is in me*, ask the children to write a poem about their best friend with the first line 'There is in you'.
- They could also write a poem about a public figure such as a politician, a singer or an actor, beginning 'There is in him/her'.
- Suggest that the children write a poem about their class, beginning 'There is in us'.
- Ask them to write a poem about their home community (village, town or street, for example), again beginning 'There is in us'.

List poems

Poetry page

The children that I know

The children that I know
are
playground warriors,
sweet singers at Christmas,
happy runners
when the holidays start.
They are
nimble gymnasts,
geographers
and historians
and, right from the heart,
poets lisping
with imperfect tongues,
and painters.
They are pet-lovers –
cats and dogs and mice;
song-lovers singing songs
with all the power
of their lungs.
They are sport-lovers.
They are rain-haters
but snow-lovers.
Hail-haters
and wind-haters.
They are skaters
and skidders
and tumblers
on winter ice.

Emily Roeves

There is in me

There is in me
a rusty sky,
a stormy night at the edge of an island,
a black, dark wood,
an army of soldiers invading, a house being bombed ...

a slice of ice
shooting across me,
a swooping roller coaster
gliding up and down.

There is in my sister
boyfriends and dressing up.
There is in my brother fighting and playing.
There is in me a terrifying, never-ending war.
There is in my father a frustrated army ...

Various children

Writing lists

Read *The children that I know* on the poetry page.

1. This is a list poem, and you are going to write one of your own. Begin by writing lists on all of the topics below, but leave an empty line between each line of your list.

All the good things people do for you.
Things you like about pets.
Things you don't like about the weather.
Things you like about weekends.
A topic of your own choice.

2. Read over your lists. Add at least one new line between each of the lines you have written. Use the examples below to give you some ideas.

I hate the wind when it blows rain into my face.

My grandma lets me stay at her house. She gives me hot chocolate when she tucks me up in bed.

Choose one of your lists and turn it into a list poem like *The children that I know*. Write it out on a separate sheet when it is finished, and draw some pictures to illustrate it.

There is in me

Read *There is in me* on the poetry page. Think about the person who is speaking in the poem, and the kind of feelings they are describing.

Think about all the different feelings you have inside you. Use the table to help you. Add some feelings of your own.

When I am playing in the team, there is in me a dragon-slayer!

When I am sad there is in me
When I am happy there is in me
When I am lonely there is in me
When I am playing in the team there is in me
When I am _____ there is in me
When I am _____ there is in me

When I am lonely there is in me an astronaut floating solitary in space.

Write *There is in me* at the top of a sheet of paper and write a list poem like the one on the poetry page. Use some of the ideas from your table, and any others you can think of.

ideas page

Shape poems

Introduction

Shape poems are an interesting poetic device that can provide lots of fun for children. Here they will be looking at a thin poem, *After Giacometti (1901–1966)* and *I'll follow you*, which is in the shape of a twisting path that someone might follow. Shape poems often use the form to reflect the subject, as these poems show, but this is not always the case. The idea, along with the syllabic ideas discussed in the chapters on haiku and cinquains, helps the children to write poems which differ visually from prose pieces.

Learning Objectives

- To appreciate that shape can contribute to the effect of a poem.
- To write shape poems.

Discussion

Read *After Giacometti* to the class, as they follow it on the sheet. The subject matter is quite advanced, but the basic idea is simple. Ask the children why it is appropriate that a poem about this artist should be shaped like this. Ask them what other subjects would be suitable for a thin poem. You could have a few objects ready: pencils, pens, chalk, string and twigs all spring readily to mind.

Activity Pages

Sculptor poems
This activity follows on from the previous chapter in that it asks the children to make a list, but this time with the specific aim of turning their list into a shape poem. The longer the list of thin things, the better. After this initial activity, ask them to make lists of thin things in different categories: nature thin things, machinery thin things, school thin things and so on.

I'll follow you
Again beginning with a list-making activity, this page guides the children through the construction of another shape poem based on following someone through different places. Suggest some useful words: under, over, behind, before, beneath, beside, beyond, inside, outside, below and so on. Include some discussion of the function of prepositions. Explain that the 'following' poem can be set anywhere, and encourage the children to make as many suggestions as they can: the supermarket, a park, the human body, under the sea, in the solar system and so on. Point out that the use of the word 'where' stops the poems becoming monotonous: 'I'll follow you/ behind the hot planet/where everything withers …'

Written Work

- The children could write thin poems with only one word per line, using an appropriate thin topic. They might make the subject appropriate – that is, about something that is thin. They could also try writing a poem where the subject matter is appropriate to the short, staccato nature of a one-word line; for example, a poem about teeth chattering in the cold, or about a fiery argument.
- The children could write a fat poem about a hippopotamus or elephant.

Performance Ideas

I'll follow you is based on Puck's speech in Shakespeare's *A Midsummer Night's Dream*:

> I'll follow you: I'll lead you about a round,
>   Through bog, through bush, through brake, through brier;
> Sometime a horse I'll be, sometime a hound,
>   A hog, a headless bear, sometime a fire;
> And neigh, and bark, and grunt, and roar, and burn,
> Like horse, hound, hog, bear, fire, at every turn.

Help the children to work out a way of performing these lines. For example, the speech could be divided up, with each child speaking a different line; they could use different tones of voice, speaking menacingly or in a friendly way. It will help if you explain that Puck is a mischievous spirit who delights in confusing people.

Thin poems

Poetry page

After Giacometti (1901–1966)

Look –
this
man
is
very,
very
thin,
but
still
standing
up –
and
I,
for
one,
believe
that
is
some
sort of
achievement.

Fred Sedgwick

I'll follow you

I'll follow you
 through the bushes,
  through the trees,
   through the flowers
    with the bees.
     I'll follow you
      through dark and light,
       through the mud,
    all through the night.
    I'll follow you
     through ice and snow.
      I'll follow high,
       I'll follow low.
        I'll follow you
       through the bushes,
        through the trees,
         through the flowers
          with the bees.

Claire, age 9

© Belair (copiable page)   BELAIR LESSON BANK – Forms of Poetry 1   33

Sculptor poems

Read *After Giacometti* on the poetry page. Giacometti was a sculptor who made very thin sculptures of people, and the poem is thin in shape, just like one of his sculptures. You are going to write some shape poems of your own.

1. Begin by making a list of thin things using the table below. Try to find a word to fill each space. Two are done for you. Continue on a separate sheet if you can.

shoelace			
lamp post			

2. On a separate sheet, turn your list of thin things into a shape poem. Here is an example.

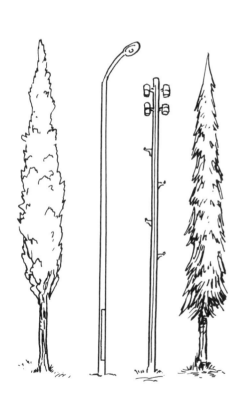

Shoe-
lace.
Tele-
graph
pole.

Lamp
post
and
twig.

Cat's
whisker,
pencil,
and
skinny
thing-
u-
-ma
jig.

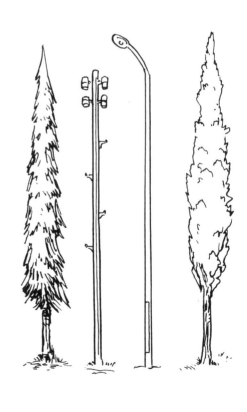

Make a list of round things and turn your list into a round shape poem.

BELAIR LESSON BANK – Forms of Poetry 1

I'll follow you

Read *I'll follow you* on the poetry page. You are going to write your own 'following' poem.

1. Begin by making a list of words that have a similar meaning to 'follow'. Fill them in on the table below. Use a thesaurus to help you.

Words that mean 'follow'

pursue			
trail			

2. Next think of some places where you might follow someone. It could be anywhere, from Saturn to the supermarket! Think of a theme for your poem and give it a title. An example is given below.

Write your own 'following' poem, giving it a shape. Use all the words you can from your list, and illustrate your poem.

ideas page

Conversation poems

Introduction

Conversation poems are of interest because they dispense with narrative and descriptive elements and leave the reader to imagine the surroundings, the appearance of the characters, even the tone of voice the speakers might use. This type of poem is ideal for performance, and the children will enjoy taking different parts to read them aloud or act them out. This can be done in pairs or as groups, with children taking turns to read the lines.

Learning Objectives

- To introduce the concept of conversation poems.
- To write a conversation poem.

Discussion

- Read *Meet-on-the-Road* aloud to the class, emphasising how the poem changes from an innocent conversation to one which is ominous. Ask the children questions: What would you have replied to Meet-on-the-Road after his first question? After his fourth? Where does the reader first realise that Meet-on-the-Road is an unpleasant character? What sort of person do the children think Meet-on-the-Road is? Though very old, this poem has disturbing modern resonances; if it is appropriate to your class, extend the discussion to include warnings against talking to strangers.
- Ask the children to describe the way they visualise Meet-on-the-Road, encouraging them to be as vivid as possible. Write key words from their descriptions on the board. Reinforce the nature and use of adjectives: a 'describing' word, a word that modifies a noun by describing a particular characteristic of it.
- Talk about what Child-as-she-stood might say to her parents, brothers and sisters and friends when she gets home.

Activity Pages

Meet-on-the-Road
Ask the children to read *Meet-on-the-Road* aloud in groups. One person could be the child while another plays Meet-on-the-Road. The rest of the group could read all the other lines ('said Child-as-she-stood'; 'said Meet-on-the-Road'). Swap roles, and read it again. Make sure everyone has a chance of being either the Child or Meet-on-the-Road. Suggest they read the poem expressing as many moods as possible: easy-going, threatening, scary, funny and so on. This should help them to understand the poem better before they complete the questions on the sheet.

Conversations and interruptions ...
Divide the children into pairs and ask them to read *Walking to watch the Town* aloud, playing the parts of father and son. Give them some ideas on 'voices' they could use, such as annoyance or amusement for the father, eagerness or impatience for the son and so on. Invite them to suggest other moods. Discuss the poem. What is the father interested in? What does the son want to talk about? Help the children to realise that the father is interested in the past, while the son wants to talk about the future. Ask the children if they have had experience of this kind of conversation with an older person.

Written Work

- Ask the children to write a conversation poem between one of the following:
  - a tree being blown about in a storm, and the wind
  - a man trying to write a poem, and his cat climbing all over his word processor
  - a woman asleep on the beach and the sea that comes in to wake her up.
- Ask the children to write their own version of *Meet-on-the-Road*, writing their own lines of dialogue, using the ideas they had during the discussion period.

Performance Ideas

Ask the children, in groups, to perform *Meet-on-the-Road* as it is written; then ask them to perform their own versions, using the dialogue they have provided for their re-worked versions.

Conversation poems
Poetry page

Meet-on-the-Road

"Now, where are you going, child?"
    Said Meet-on-the-Road.
"To school, sir, to school, sir,"
    Said Child-as-she-stood.

"What have you got in your bag, child?"
    Said Meet-on-the-Road.
"My dinner, sir, my dinner, sir,"
    Said Child-as-she-stood.

"What have you got for your dinner, child?"
    Said Meet-on-the-Road.
"Some brown bread and cheese, sir,"
    Said Child-as-she-stood.

"Oh, then, give me some, right now,"
    Said Meet-on-the-Road.
"I've little enough for myself, sir,"
    Said Child-as-she-stood.

"What have you got that coat on for?"
    Said Meet-on-the-Road.
"To keep the wind and chill from me, sir,"
    Said Child-as-she-stood.

"I wish the wind would blow through you,"
    Said Meet-on-the-Road.
"Oh, what a wish, what a wish!"
    Said Child-as-she-stood.

"What are those bells ringing for?"
    Said Meet-on-the-Road.
"To ring bad spirits home again, sir,"
    Said Child-as-she-stood.

"Oh then, I must be going, child!"
    Said Meet-on-the-Road.
"So fare you well, so fare you well, sir,"
    Said Child-as-she-stood.

Traditional

Meet-on-the-Road

Read *Meet-on-the-Road* on the poetry page. This is a conversation poem. It's also a little bit scary! You are going to write your own poem in the form of a conversation between someone like you, and someone – or something – a little bit scary...

1. The poem doesn't say what Meet-on-the-Road looks like, so use your imagination! What do you think he looks like? What might he wear? How might he sound? Jot down your ideas below.

What I think Meet-on-the-Road is like

2. Now think of someone or something you would *not* like to meet on the road. It might be a fire-breathing dragon, or an alien, or a giant. On a separate sheet, make some notes about what your Meet-on-the-Road is like. Think about what you might say to each other.

Write your conversation poem. It doesn't have to be as long as *Meet-on-the-Road*, but it should include a conversation. Then draw a picture of your Meet-on-the-Road.

Conversations and interruptions ...

Read this poem.

Walking to watch the Town

Father	It was a day like this, I still remember. I walked with my dad through red dusty leaves –	Father	Better, Son. They were brilliant. And they took The country by storm, they beat the lot. United. City. Arsenal. The lot. And that day, the day we thrashed –
Son	And kicked them up like this, and this and this?	Son	Dad?
Father	Yes, Son. I'm telling you. And Town Ran out that day – I can see them now –	Father	Yes, Son?
Son	Did they wear blue and white, then, Dad? I hope they've always been the Superblues!	Son	Dad, will we win today?
Father	They did. Let me tell you, that day –	Father	Who knows, Son? But It was a day like this, thirty years ago, When me and my dad walked to watch the Town –
Son	– and Dad?	Son	Did you hold his hand, Dad, like I'm holding yours?
Father	Yes, Son?	Father	Reckon I did ... It was a day like this –
Son	Were they good, like they are now?		

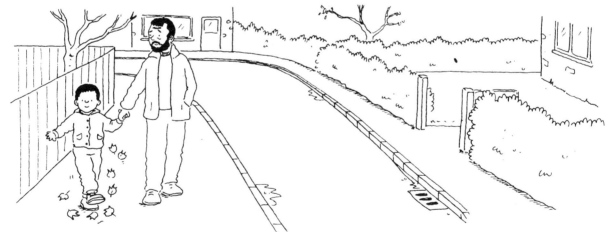

1. Read the poem out loud in your groups. Think about how the father and son would sound. Would one speak more quickly than the other? Would one sound more excited than the other?

2. Think of someone you know, such as a parent or grandparent, who sometimes talks about things you find a bit boring! Imagine a conversation with this person, and make some notes on what it might be like.

 Write your own conversation poem. Make it as natural as possible, with interruptions, just like in real life!

ideas page

Epitaphs

Introduction

In *Does it have to Rhyme?* the author Sandy Brownjohn says that an epitaph 'comments on the person's life, character ... profession or manner of death, and often incorporates a play on words'. This exercise introduces children to the concept of epitaphs as a form of poetry, focusing on the characteristics of the subject. Throughout, the activity pages stress that epitaphs frequently include poking fun at the subject, but the children are asked to be gently mocking rather than unkind.

Learning Objectives

- To introduce the concept of epitaphs.
- To write an epitaph.

Discussion

- Explain to the children what an epitaph is, then read the three epitaphs on the poetry page aloud to the class. Discuss how an epitaph might begin: some suggestions are 'Here lies ...', 'Beneath this ground/stone ...', 'Under your feet ...' and so on. Mention the characters in a novel you all know, possibly the one you are reading to the class. What might they put in an epitaph for the BFG or Long John Silver? Extend the discussion to figures from history with whom the children are familiar. What might they put in an epitaph for Henry VIII, a Viking raider or Florence Nightingale?
- Using an appropriate degree of sensitivity, talk to the children about any pets they have owned that are now dead. Discuss the animals and their habits and characteristics, writing some of the children's observations on the board. Then arrange their comments into epitaphs, asking for more suggestions from the class. They can compose epitaphs for:
    – a dog
    – a cat
    – a hamster
    or any other animals they have owned.

Activity Pages

Irritating habits
Begin by having a class discussion on irritating habits, encouraging ideas from the children. Then help them to compile their lists of irritating habits. Point out how the word 'talked' is frequently repeated in the poem about the gardener, and suggest they use this repetitive device for emphasis in their epitaphs.

Working lives
To help the children think about what someone might do during their working day, begin with making a list of things a teacher does, inviting suggestions from the children and writing them up on the board. Then extend the discussion to the fantasy figures in the exercise.

Written Work

- Ask the children to write an epitaph with one word repeated many times. Suggest some titles, such as *Epitaph on a worrier* or *Epitaph on a door-slammer*. Give them this example:
    He slammed the kitchen door,
    he slammed the garage door,
    he slammed the car door,
    at dead of night.
    Now he's slammed down
    by a coffin lid,
    he slams no more,
    and all is quiet.
- Ask the children to write an epitaph on an historical or fictional figure, reminding them of the discussion you had earlier. Their epitaph should focus on the person's actions during their lifetime.
- Write a list of occupations on the board; for example:
    – teacher
    – priest
    – doctor
    – bus-driver
    – nurse
    – ballet-dancer
    – zoo-keeper.
Invite suggestions from the children. Ask them to write a list of things these people might do daily in their job. Then ask the children to choose one of these and write an epitaph for them.

Epitaphs
Poetry page

On King Charles the Second

Here lies our sovereign lord the King
Whose promise none relies on;
He never said a foolish thing,
Nor ever did a wise one.

John Wilmot, Earl of Rochester, 1647–1680

Epitaph on a talkative gardener

He talked and talked and talked and talked.
He talked while he stood, he talked while he walked.
He talked while he ate, he talked while he drank.
He talked while he thrived, he talked as he sank.
He talked while hoeing, he talking while forking ...
Listen hard now. You can still hear him talking.

Fred Sedgwick

On a central defender

He has headed his last own goal
from the edge of the area,
pulled the last shirt
of a speedy striker.
He has called for his last offside –
his arm in the air like an aerial –
and gone to his final early bath.

Fred Sedgwick

Irritating habits

Read *Epitaph on a talkative gardener* on the poetry page. The gardener clearly talked a lot! Epitaphs reflect a person's life, and sometimes they talk about a person's irritating habits.

1. You are going to write an epitaph about someone with an irritating habit. Start by making a list of your 'Top ten irritating habits'. Think of things that really annoy you, like people making a noise when they chew gum.

My top ten irritating habits

1. _____
2. _____
3. _____
4. _____
5. _____
6. _____
7. _____
8. _____
9. _____
10. _____

2. Pick one of these and imagine someone who might have that irritating habit. What did he or she do for a living? How old were they? How often did they practise their habit? On a separate sheet write as many notes as you can about this imaginary person. Draw a picture of them to go with your notes.

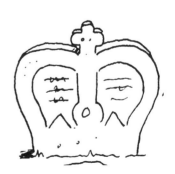

 Write your epitaph. Remember, it shouldn't be too long, as it has to fit on a headstone. It shouldn't be too unkind, but you can poke a little fun!

Working lives

Read *Epitaph on a central defender* on the poetry page. The epitaph talks about the things the footballer did while he played. It doesn't sound as if he was very good at his job!

1. You are going to write an epitaph for someone who was loved by his or her friends, but who wasn't very good at their job. For each person mentioned below, make a list of two things they might do in their job that might go wrong. An example is done for you.

An inventor...	An explorer...	A vampire...
Things that might go wrong	Things that might go wrong	Things that might go wrong
1. might get blown up	1. might get lost	1. might be vegetarian
2. _____	2. _____	2. _____
3. _____	3. _____	3. _____

2. Think of a character of your own who isn't very good at what they do. On a separate sheet, make a list of what might go wrong for them.

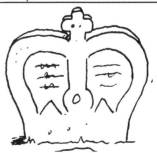

 Choose one of the characters and write your epitaph. Make it as funny as you can – but remember not to be unkind!

Free verse

ideas page

Introduction

Free verse, as its name indicates, allows considerable freedom in its composition because it is untrammelled by rules of metre or rhyme; however, this does not mean that it is not a poetic device with its own conventions. It is not something which can be 'flung together', and the children should revise their free verse poems as much as any others they have written. Free verse needs to consist of evocative, vivid prose and each word must work for its living. Children should find free verse relatively simple to understand and write; cats provide a good subject because they lend themselves to poetic description and most children will have had some experience of them.

Learning Objectives

- To use observational faculties to devise metaphors and similes.
- To construct a free verse poem incorporating metaphors and similes.

Discussion

- Although pictures or videos (or even, conceivably, a real cat) could be used for this exercise, the children should be able to conjure up mental images strong enough to produce the required imagery. Ask the children to close their eyes and imagine a cat, preferably one they know. Tell them to look at it hard with their mind's eye, while their physical eyes have a rest. They should look at the cat's fur, and remember what it feels like when they stroke it, and look at the cat's back as it moves against their leg. Ask them to imagine the cat as it stalks something in the garden, or creeps under the gate. Can they look into its mouth as it yawns, or laps milk? What shapes can they see in its mouth? What are the teeth like?
- Explain the nature of metaphors and similes, so that the children are aware of the distinction; remind them that similes usually use the word 'like', while a metaphor describes one thing in terms of another. Give some examples.

Activity Pages

Metaphors and similes
Read through the examples. Discuss how the curled-up cat is compared to a shell, and how well this works as a comparison. Ask the children to use the examples and think of their own metaphors and similes for each picture. Emphasise that there is no right or wrong answer.

More metaphors and similes
This focuses on specific parts of the cat. Ask the children to think about the cat's open mouth. What shapes can they see on the top of the mouth? What shapes are the teeth? What colours can they see in the mouth? Talk about the texture of things: the tongue, for example. Ask them to think of words to describe what the fur, tongue and ears feel like. Ask them to describe the pads on the cat's paws. Does the sound of a cat purring or mewing remind them of anything? Focusing on the sense of touch, talk about what a cat's fur or nose feels like. Can they describe the experience of being scratched by a cat, or licked by one?

Written Work

- Suggest that the children begin their poem by writing it out as a piece of prose. They can then break it up into a free verse form by beginning a new line when they naturally pause for breath, or simply when it 'feels' right to start a new line.
- Suggest they write a free verse poem about another animal, either wild or domestic.
- Give the children a prose passage, preferably from a book you have been reading as a class. Ask them to turn it into a free verse poem, experimenting with different line lengths and layouts.
- Do the same with a text-book, challenging the children to turn, for example, a maths problem into a poem, or a scientific definition into a poem.

Free verse

Poetry page

Looking at a cat 1

The cat's eyes are olive green.
The shape is like a kiwi fruit.
She walks slowly
like a Sioux Indian searching for food.
She strides
like the most important person
in the world.
She curls up
like an old football with a dangly bit.
The tongue curls up like a ball.

Alice, age 10

Looking at a cat 2

Big green marbles
are stuck in the middle
of a mass of black fur.
He is a Gurkha stalking,
running, jumping and bouncing.
He's got springs
on the bottoms of his paws.
He pounces,
a glider taking off.
When he arches his back
he is a black rainbow.

Alan, age 10

Metaphors and similes

Read the poems on the poetry page. Both the poems are in free verse, which means they do not rhyme or follow a metre. In free verse, metaphors and similes are very important.

Look at these cats and read the sentences below.

Tick the box to show whether the sentence is a simile or a metaphor. Then see if you can match the correct simile or metaphor to the picture. Write the number of the sentence in the box in the picture.

1. The big cat is like my worst nightmare.	metaphor		simile
2. The cat is like a diver.	metaphor		simile
3. The cat is a shell on the beach of the carpet.	metaphor		simile

 Think of one metaphor and one simile for each of the following cats.

Metaphor:

Simile:

Metaphor:

Simile:

More metaphors and similes

You are going to write your own free verse poem. You will be using lots of metaphors and similes.

1. Begin by thinking of some metaphors and similes to go with the pictures below. An example is done for you.

| When she hunts, the cat's paw | When the cat lies in my arms his body | The cat's tongue is like | The cat's ears are like |

is a velvet bag full of knives.

2. Think about a cat you have seen. Then think about the different shapes you can see in the cat. What colours can you see? Fill in the table with ideas of your own, using similes and metaphors. An example is done for you.

The cat's eyes are burning opal coals.
The cat's teeth _____
The cat's tail _____
The cat's back _____
The cat's whiskers _____
The cat's legs _____

 Write your free verse poem. Use some of the similes and metaphors you have thought of, and add some new ones if you can.

Glossary

alliteration The use of the same consonant at the beginning of each word, as in 'Peter Piper picked a peck of pickled pepper.'

cinquain A five-line poem with two syllables in the first line, four in the second, six in the third, eight in the fourth and two in the fifth.

cliché A word or expression that has lost its force from overuse.

epitaph A commemorative speech or inscription on a gravestone, or a final judgement on a person or thing.

free verse Non-rhyming poetry with no metrical pattern.

haiku A Japanese verse form with 17 syllables, five in the first line, seven in the second and five in the third.

metaphor A figure of speech implying a comparison between two things where no literal similarity exists; for example, 'the ship ploughs the sea' implies a comparison between a ship and a plough.

onomatopoeia Words that imitate the sound they describe, such as babble, buzz or hiss.

pun The use of words in such a way as to exploit ambiguities of meaning for humorous effect.

riddle A question or verse designed to be a puzzle, requiring some effort to understand its meaning.

simile A figure of speech expressing the resemblance of one thing to another, introduced by 'like' or 'as'.

stanza A verse of a poem.

The following books may be useful reading:

The Exeter Riddle Book, translated by Kevin Crossley-Holland, published by Penguin.

The New Exeter Book of Riddles, edited by Kevin Crossley-Holland and Lawrence Sail, published by Enitharmon.

The Mad Parrot's Countdown, by John Mole, published by Peterloo.

The Conjurer's Rabbit, by John Mole, published by Blackie.

The Orchard Book of Funny Poems, by Wendy Cope, published by Orchard Books.